Debbie MacKinnon trained as a medical and scientific illustrator at Hornsey College in London. She worked in publishing as an art director, first at Dorling Kindersley, and later at Frances Lincoln. Currently a freelance designer and writer specializing in children's books, she has three children of her own.

Anthea Sieveking has been a successful photographer for many years, and is well-known for her photographs of children and babies. Her previous books include *The Macmillan Guide to Child Health*, *The Encyclopedia of Pregnancy and Birth*, *The Baby's Book of Babies*, *How Many?*, *What's Inside?*, *What Colour?* and *What Shape?*

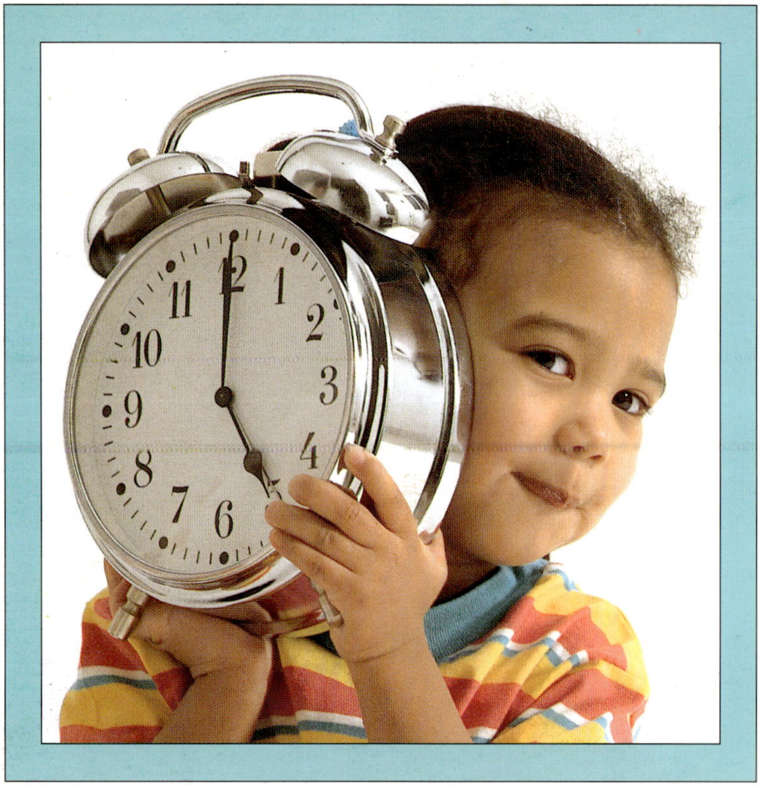

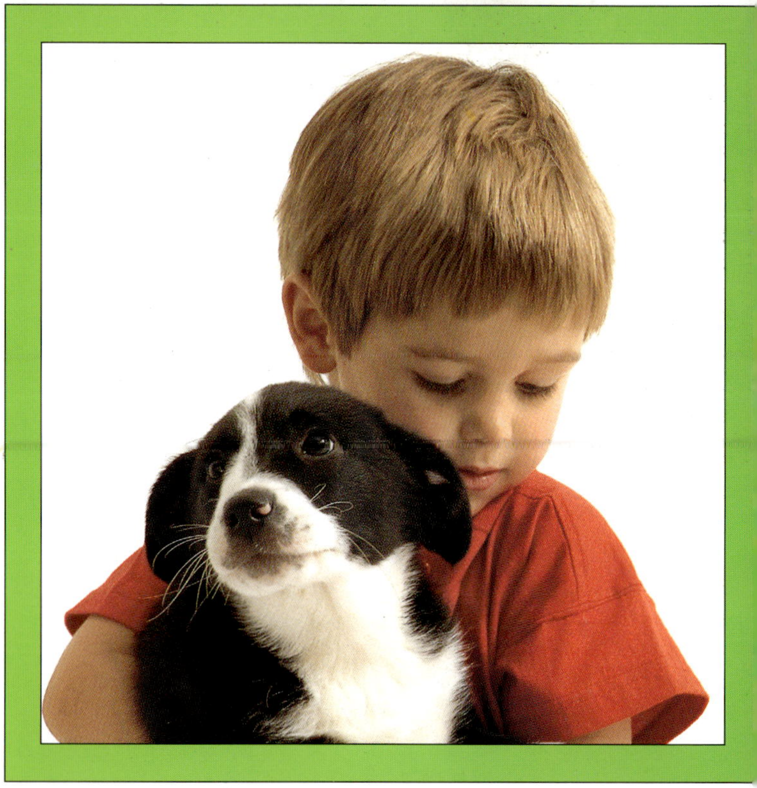

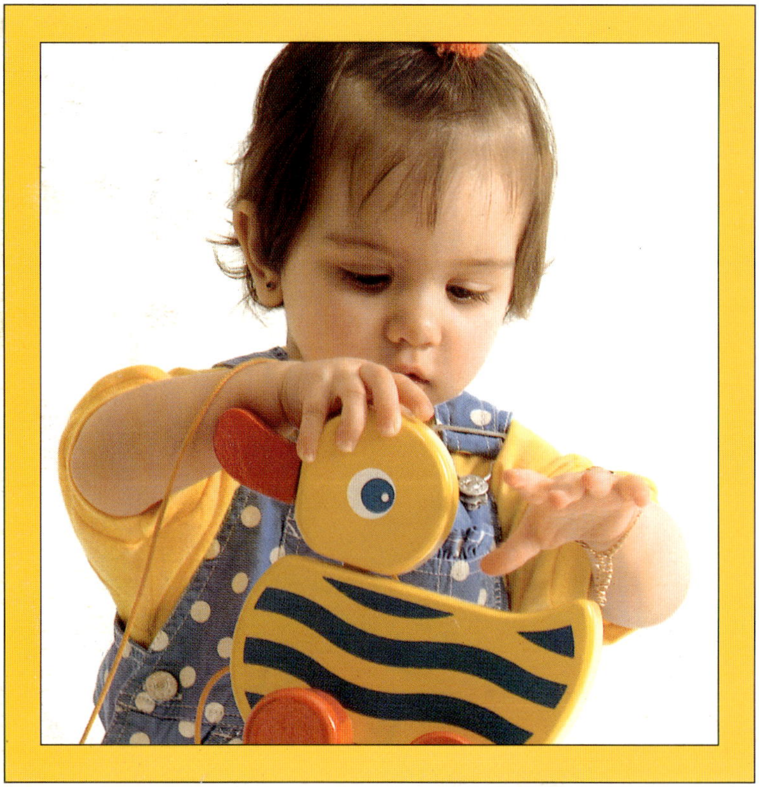

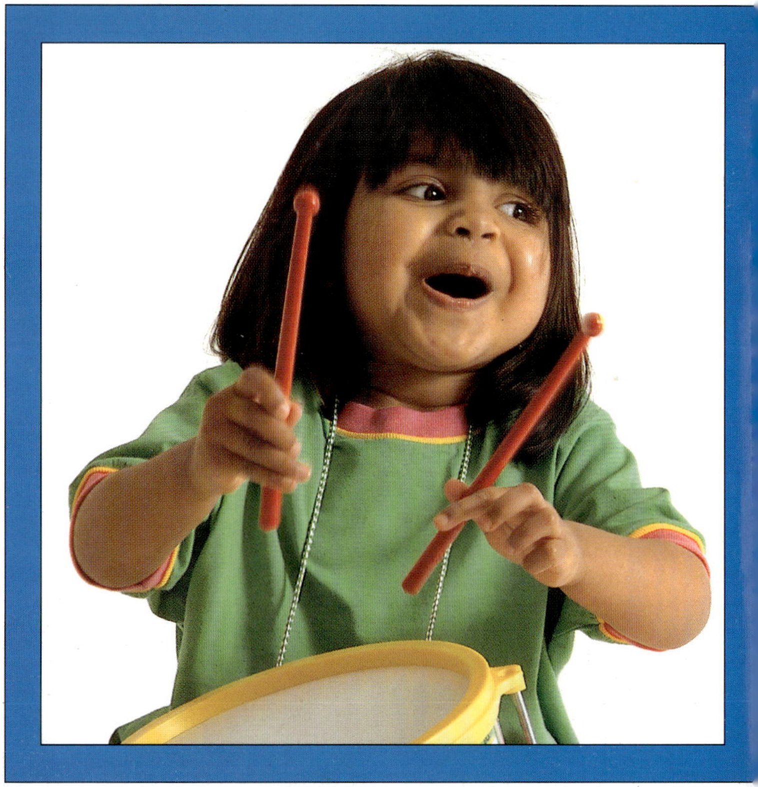

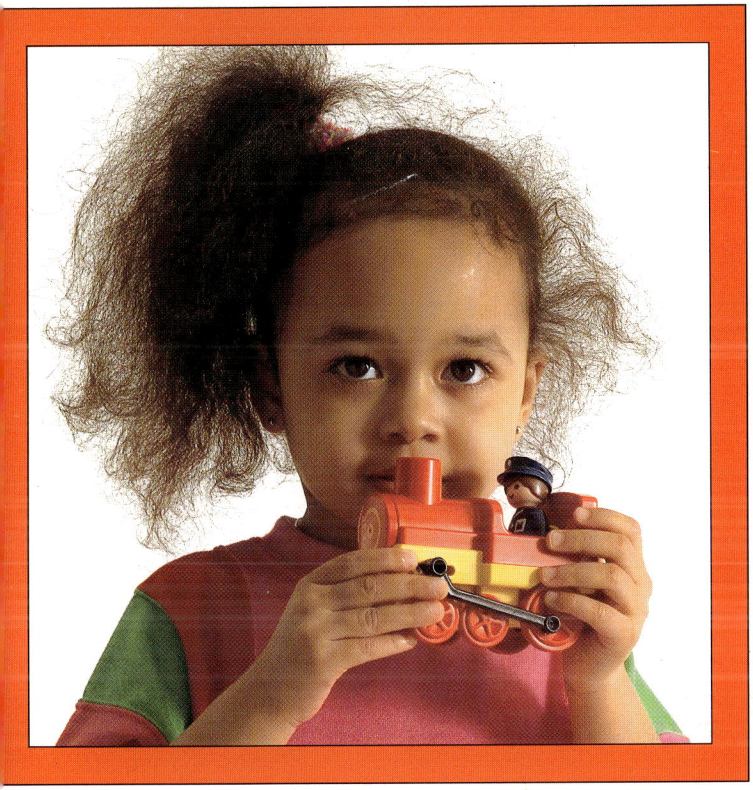
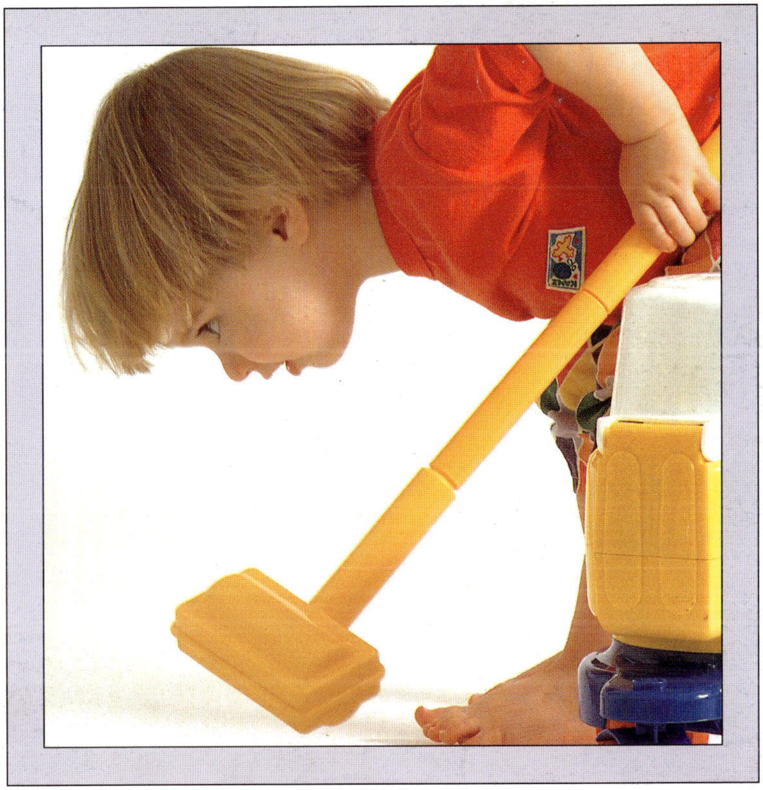
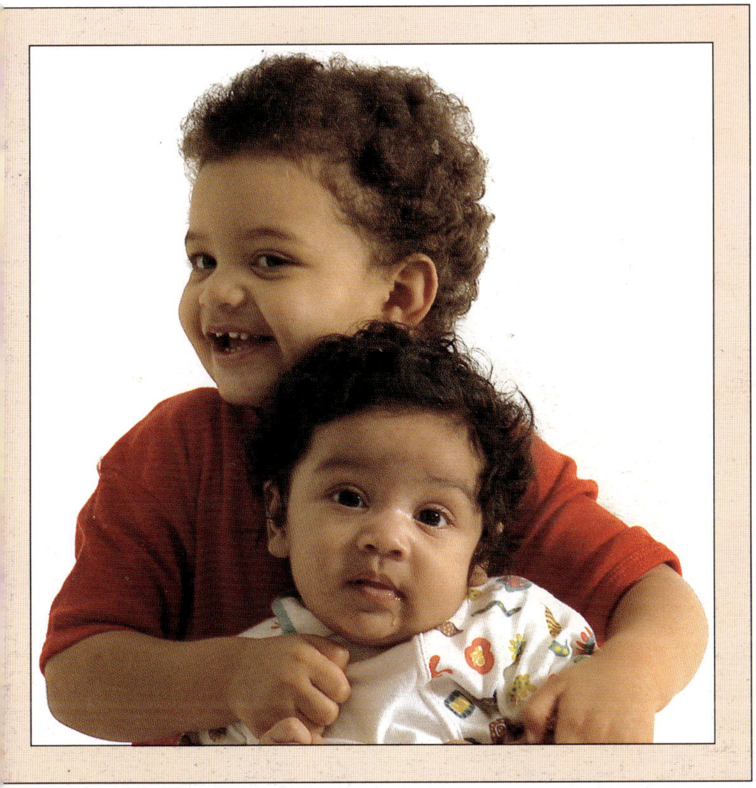
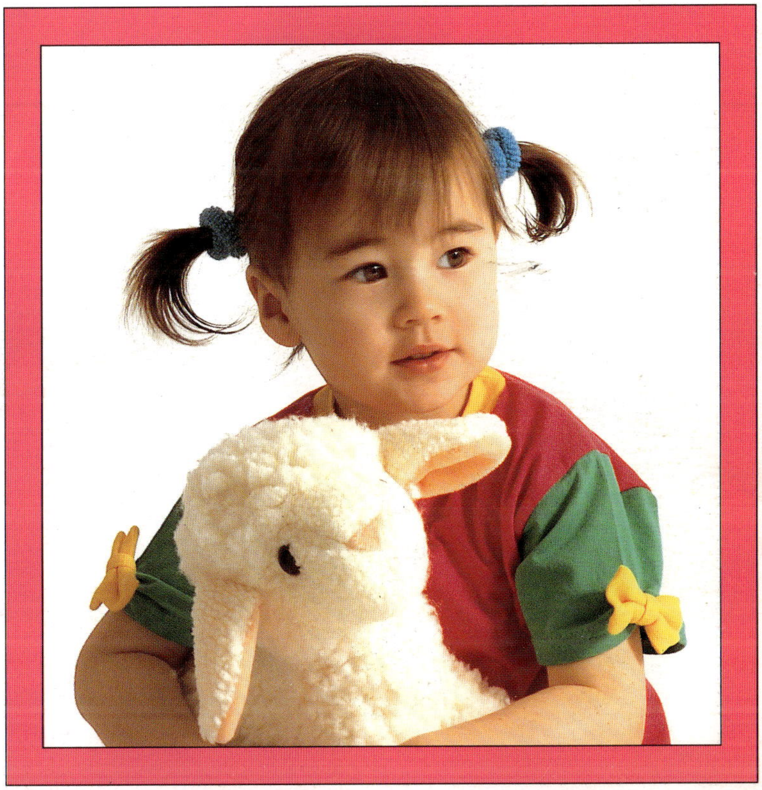

For my noisy family – D.M.
For Tom and Harriet – A.S.

What Noise? copyright © Frances Lincoln Limited 1993
Text copyright © Debbie MacKinnon 1993
Photographs copyright © Anthea Sieveking 1993

First published in Great Britain in 1993 by
Frances Lincoln Limited, 4 Torriano Mews
Torriano Avenue, London NW5 2RZ

First paperback edition 1996

All rights reserved.
No part of this publication may be reproduced, stored in a retrieval system, or transmitted, in any form, or by any means, electrical, mechanical, photocopying, recording or otherwise without the prior written permission of the publisher or a licence permitting restricted copying. In the United Kingdom such licences are issued by the Copyright Licensing Agency, 90 Tottenham Court Road, London W1P 9HE.

British Library Cataloguing in Publication Data available on request.

ISBN 0-7112-0806-9 hardback
ISBN 0-7112-1138-8 paperback

Printed in Hong Kong

Design and Art Direction: Debbie MacKinnon

3 5 7 9 8 6 4 2

WHAT NOISE?

Debbie MacKinnon
Photographs by Anthea Sieveking

FRANCES LINCOLN

What noise does Samuel's dog make?

woof! woof!

more pets

tweet tweet tweet

wheep wheep

miaow!
purrr purrr

ee-ee-ee

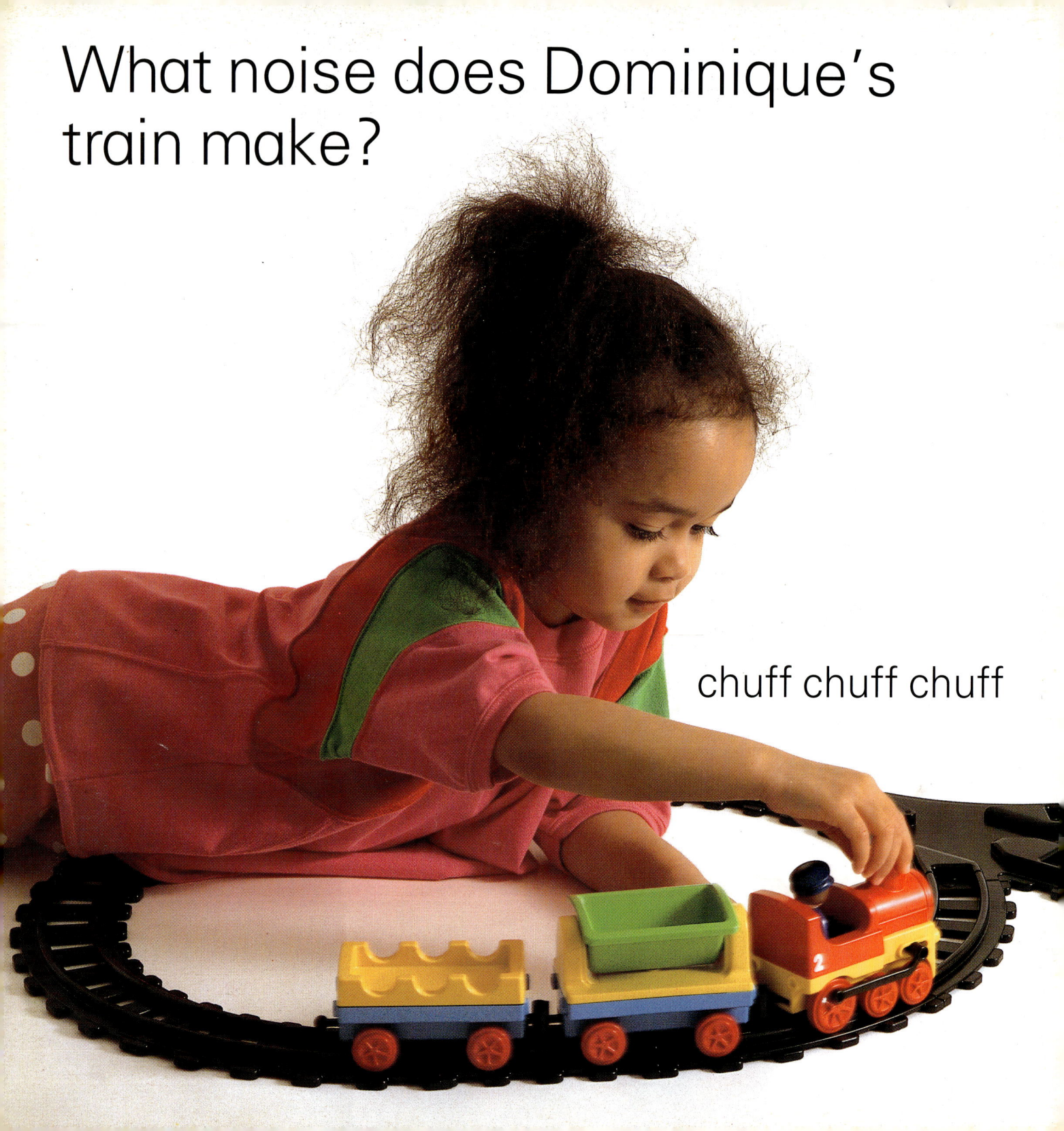

What noise does Dominique's train make?

chuff chuff chuff

more things that go

whirrrrrrrrr

vrrrm vrrrm!

chug chug

brrrm brrrm!

What noise does Francesca's duck make?

quack quack!

more birds

Pretty Polly!
squawk

cheep
cheep
cheep

cock-a-doodle-DOO!

tu-whit tu-whoo!

What noise does Grace's alarm clock make?

clang-a-lang-a-lang-a-lang!

more clocks

tick-tock
tick-tock

dong!
dong!
dong!

cuckoo!
cuckoo!

peep-peep
peep-peep

What noise does Anna's lamb make?

baaa! baaa!

more animals

neighhh!

hee-haw!

mooo!

oink oink!

What noise does Joshua's vacuum cleaner make?

varoooooom!

more machines

zzzeeeeeeeee

brrr-brrr
brrr-brrr

whizzzzzz

click

What noise does Rosie's drum make?

boom boom!

boom boom!

more music

toot toot

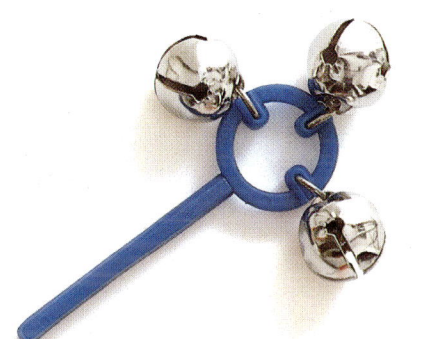

ting-a-ling-a-ling

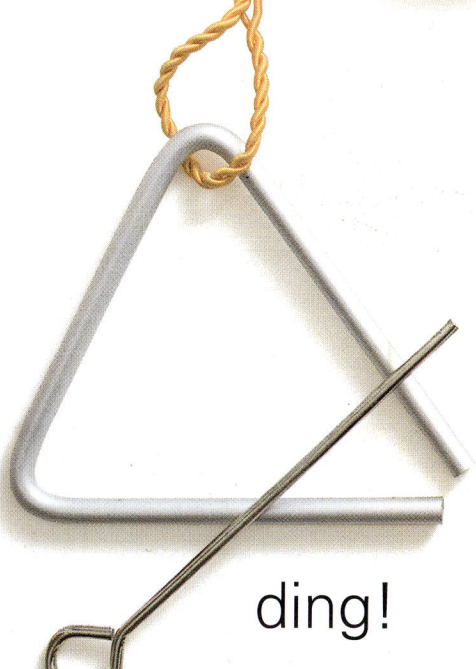

ding!

crash! crash!

What noise does Daniel's baby sister make?

hee hee!
ha ha ha!

more babies

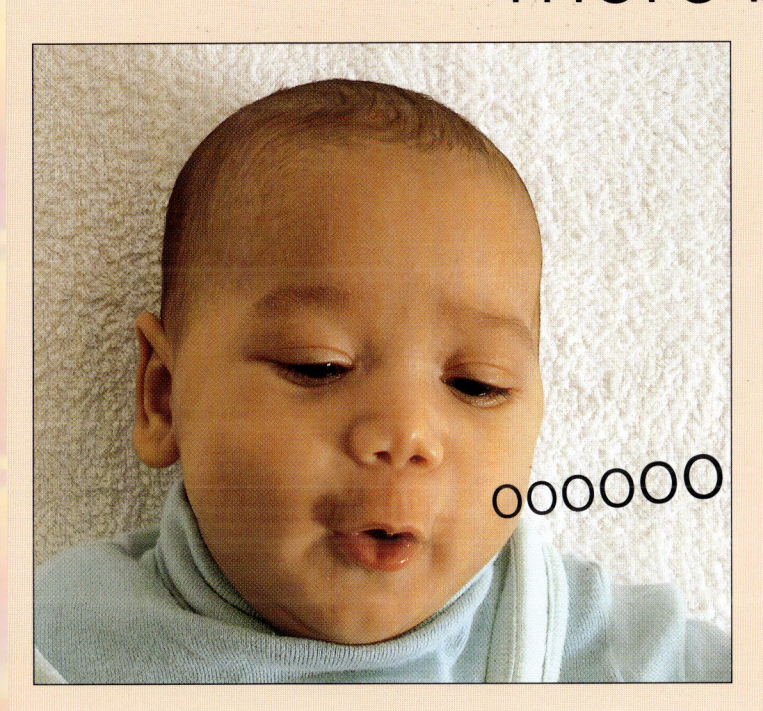

oooooo

ga
ga
ga
gooo

waaaaaa!

zzzz-zzzz

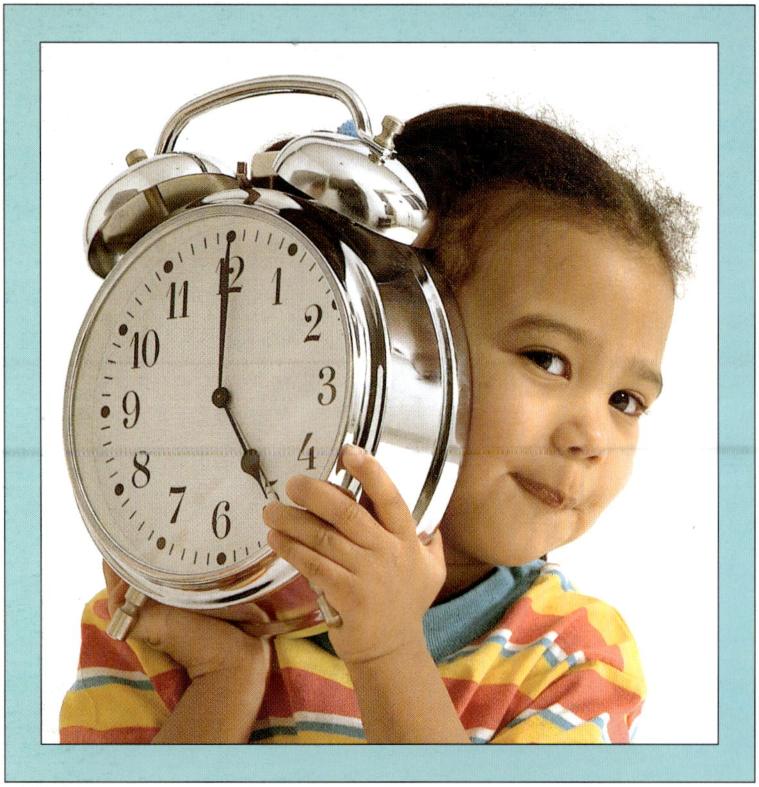
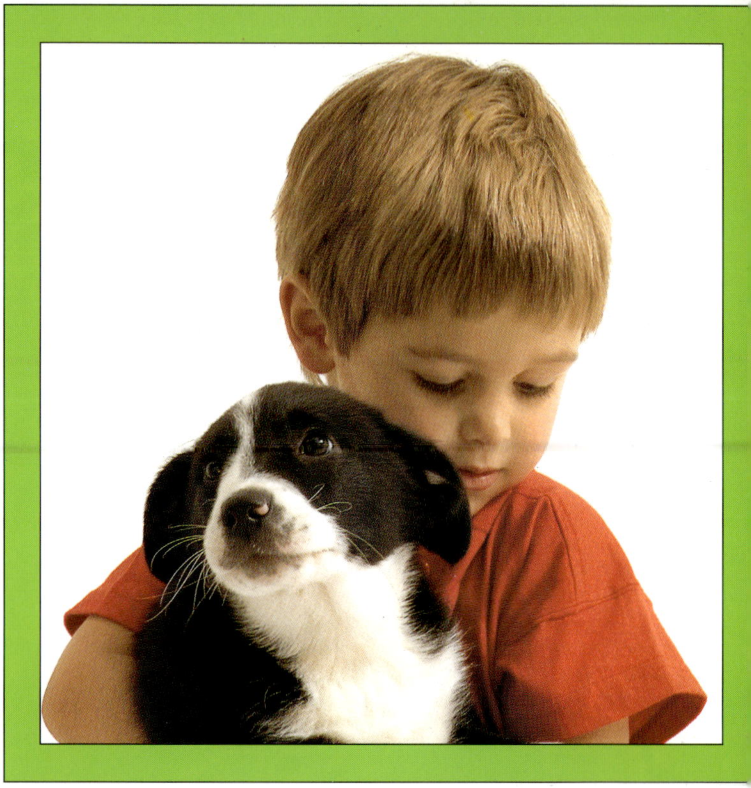
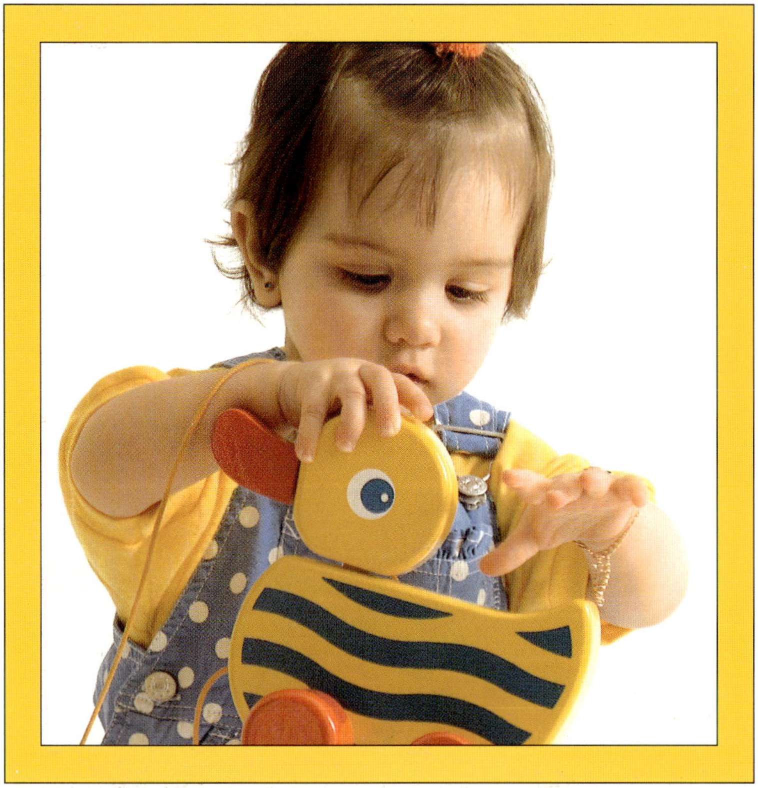
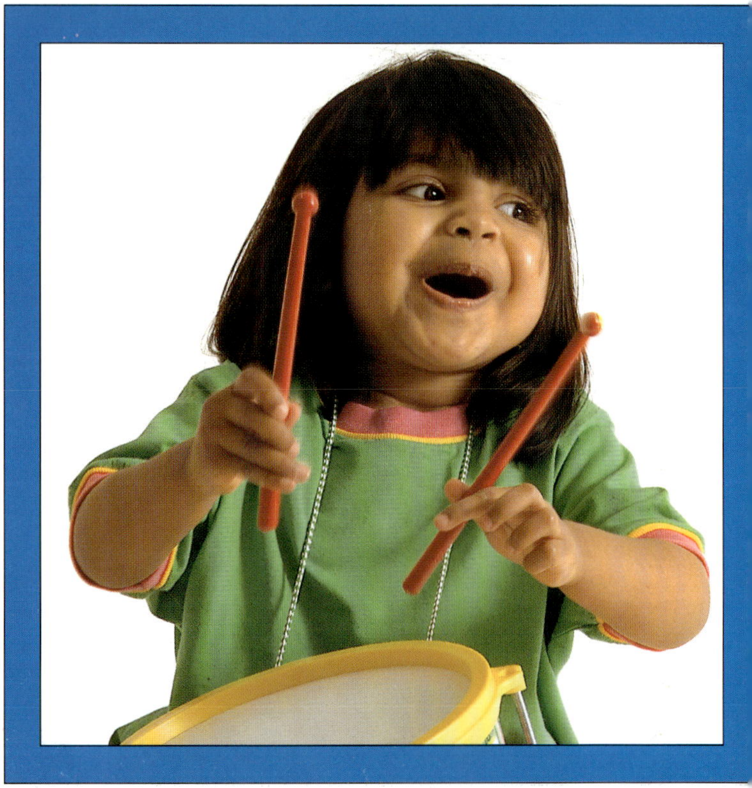

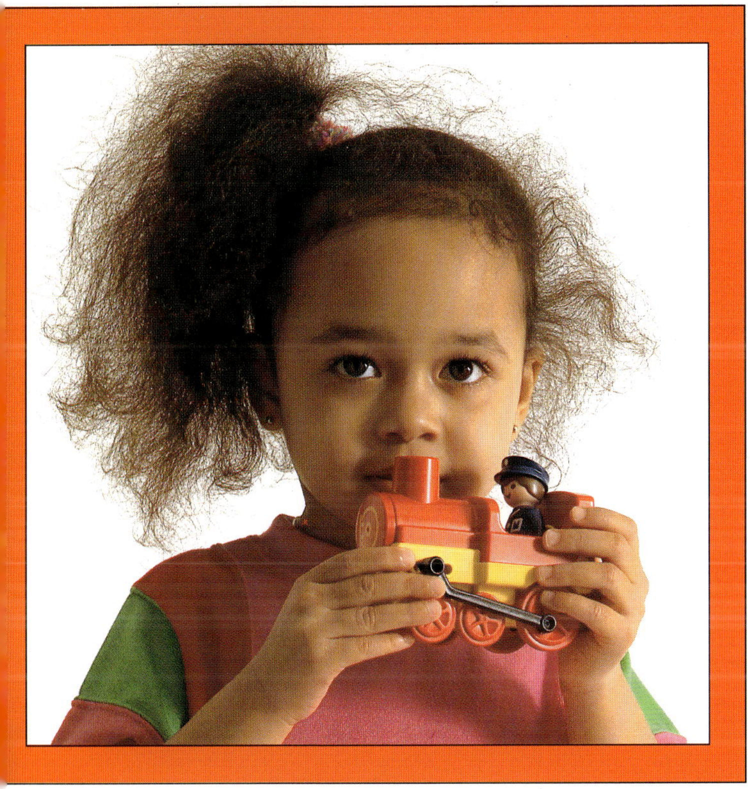
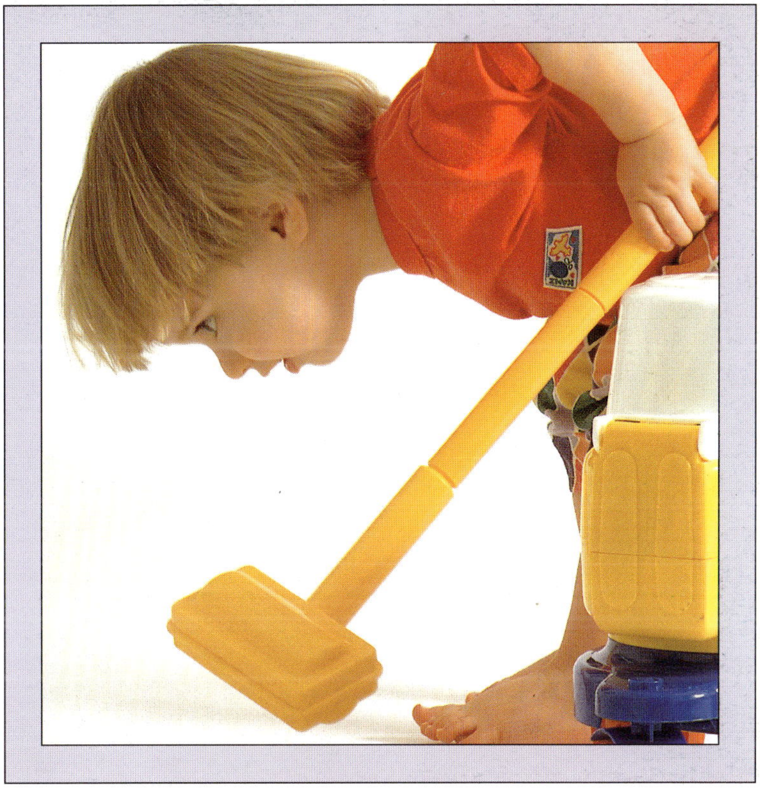
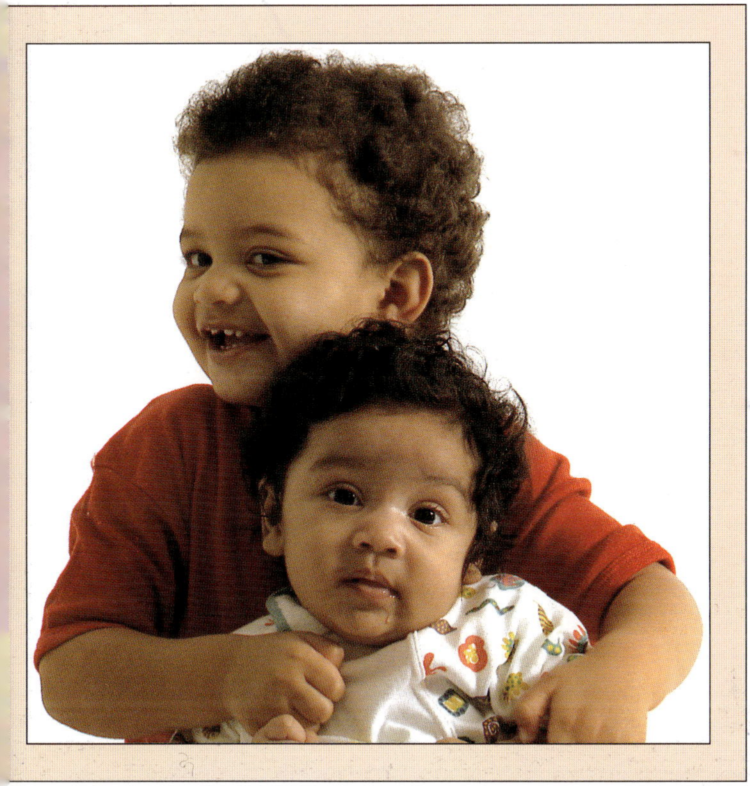
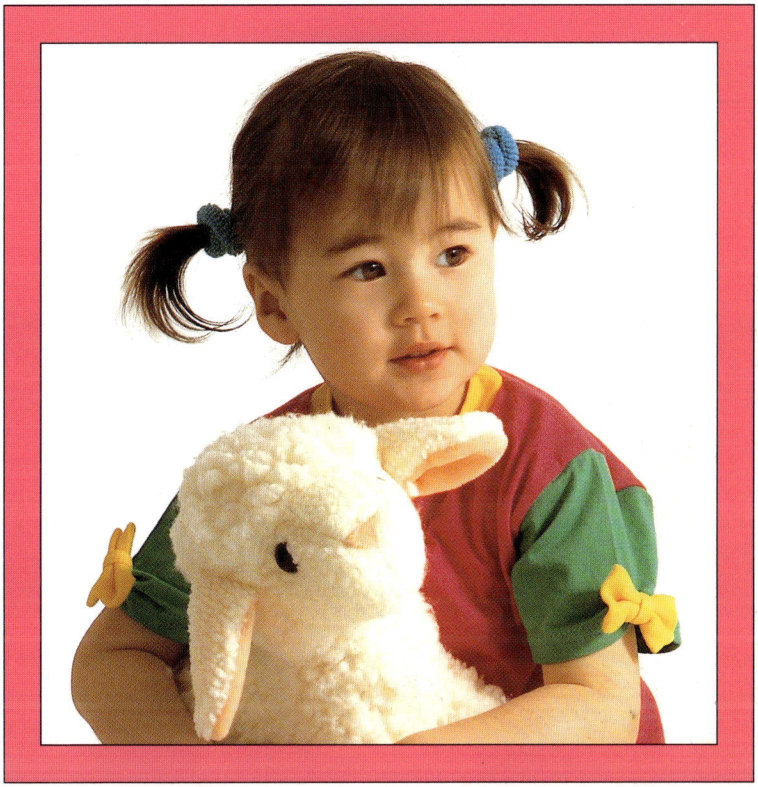

MORE BOOKS IN PAPERBACK FROM FRANCES LINCOLN

THE BABY'S BOOK OF BABIES
Kathy Henderson
Photographs by Anthea Sieveking

Babies, babies everywhere! Here are all kinds of babies, up to their antics, in lots of familiar everyday scenes - ideal for parents and toddlers to share.

'A perfect introduction to the world of books' *School Librarian*

Suitable for Nursery Level

ISBN 0-7112-0773-9

MY FIRST ABC
Debbie MacKinnon
Photographs by Anthea Sieveking

From Abby's apple to Zack's zebra, this lively ABC of toddlers in bright, beautiful photographs is perfect for the very young. An enjoyable way to the learn the alphabet.

Suitable for Nursery Level

ISBN 0-7112-0897-2

FIDDLE-I-FEE
Jakki Wood

An exuberant retelling of a well-known nursery rhyme that will have children singing along in no time. Margaret Lion has arranged the accompanying melody, based on a traditional folk song, for piano and guitar.

Suitable for National Curriculum English - Reading, Key Stage 1
Scottish Guidelines English Language - Reading, Level A

ISBN 0-7112-0860-3

Frances Lincoln titles are available from all good bookshops.